STAY TIL SUNRISE

STAY TIL SUNRISE

LAUREN E RATHJENS

To Mom and Dad-
Thank you. For everything.

A Note from the Author...

Hello dear reader. I never thought the day would come when I would write to you. This book has been a labor of love for the past 5 years and these poems have been my lifeline. Now I am passing them on to you. I wrote some of these poems at rock bottom. I wrote some of these poems when I felt on top of the world. I wrote them on receipts and journal pages, typed them in my note's app, and scribbled them on the backs of essays handed back.

During the timeframe of this book being written, I experienced some of my lowest lows and my highest highs. I fell in love. I went to residential treatment. I laughed. I cried. I survived even the worst days. I feel as though I am giving a part of myself away to you in these pages, but I am ready to let this part of my story go out into the world.

Remember, dear reader, that you are not what happened to you. You are not your demons. You are not the thoughts that plague you in the middle of the night. You are so much more. And your life means more than you could ever imagine. I know it sounds cheesy, and maybe you are at a place in life where this feels like mockery of your pain. It's not. I have published some of my darkest thoughts here to let you know that you are not alone. You are never alone.

Thank you for your love and support and thank you for helping me live my dreams. I hope you love it. I hope you feel seen. But most of all, I hope that it gives you hope.

All the love,
Lauren

Part One: Midnight

*I have forgotten what my own name tastes like
when I say it out loud*

　　Driving at night in the rain
Screaming a song from a shared playlist
Used to be my favorite activity
Until my passenger seat became perpetually empty
And the burn in my throat from yelling at traffic lights to turn
Is now the only way I know I'm alive
　　I don't feel the tears til they have soaked my shirt
And even then, they are just a reminder of my sadness
I have ticket stubs in my car from shitty tinder dates,
Mixtapes from people I haven't spoken to in months,
Smiley faces drawn in backroad dust form people
I have long since driven away from
　　Sometimes I sit in empty parking lots and press play
Just to feel like I have someone beside me again

The fear of failing in recovery hunts me down
Like a pack of wolves
They prey on my anxiety
And track me down by my anguished cries
    I am running through the night-
Crawling on bloodied hands and knees
    Fatigued, hungry, in constant pain
Yet their owling is constantly closing in
With each stumble I make
    And so I run.

Swimming in sadness
Is the drowning I have
Always known
Treading water my whole life
Just to stay afloat
Being pulled out by the riptide
Caught in the undertow
Too far out for my feet to touch
    Sinking to the bottom
    Let me go.

4 am
Following a spiral
Down
Down
Down
Crying to a darkness I have come to
Know
Huddled in the middle of the night,
Lights off,
Music on
Sadness swallows me
Until I am nothing but a memory,
One you think of when you look
To the night sky
They say when you see a star in our universe
Its been dead for thousands of years
I don't know why
But I feel myself fading,
Too
The person you see is already gone,
So look up at the cosmos
And make a wish
As I
Slip
Into
The
Night

Sometimes, it feels like the sadness is all I have left.
There is a hollowness where my smile should be
And a chasm in the place inside my rib cage
Where my heart should beat
    I wonder if one day they will find these midnight musings
I have compiled
And asked themselves
How they could have missed it,
    How I could have slipped away beneath their very feet
Like the tide returning to the sea.

Fill the bathtub to the brim,
Watch your skin redden
In the sweltering heat
Count the drips from the faucet
    Feel the sweat draw lines
Down your back
Close your eyes
And picture that you are
Anywhere
But here
    Hold your breath
Dive beneath the surface
Listen to the sound of your heartbeat
Under water
    Pretend you still believe in God
Wash your feet of your own sins
Seek control in the confinements
Of a bathtub
Count back from ten
    Forget what made you feel dirty
In the first place.

Lies.
I am beautiful when I am broken-
When I am spilling out of every inch
Of my pleading body
On hands and knees,
Fingernails bloodied,
Dragging myself forward by the small hope for a better tomorrow
I am beautiful when I am weak-
When the tears wet my cheeks like rain
And I call you just to hear you breathe.
I am beautiful when I am on the edge of life and death,
Where my manic pixie fantasies come true,
Where I close my eyes while driving just to see
How far I can go,
I am beautiful when I am falling apart-
When I am grasping for things to hold onto.
    I wish I was beautiful when the sunshine hits my face
And the shadows dissipate,
But I'm not.
    I am nothing without my illness;
An artist without a muse.
How sick of me to feed on my own misery.
At least then, while devouring my sadness by the handfuls,

I feel beautiful.

There is a heaviness behind my eyes,
One part sadness,
Two parts fatigue
My dreams keep me awake in the night,
Playing out scenarios with people
Whose names my tongue long ago buried
To feel as though I am temporary
To all the people that I see as permanent
Is crimson cracked knuckles
From fists held too tightly
Pressing palms against my eyes
So deep heat burns inside my head
    I think of all the ways a person can be dead and still standing
I have found that being the one who has known all
But been known by none
Will do just that.

It is 3:48 am and the numbness that has been holding me hostage
Is keeping any tears from falling.
Even though my stomach is a roaring sea,
And my head feels like firecrackers are being
Shot off in every direction
I don't know if it's the pills
Or if I have just been pulling myself along for too long
But my world has become a dull room with
A population of one
Any emotion existing outside of the spectrum
Of a baseline of emptiness is not accepted
Too scared to feel anything that might lead to being let down
Too worried about not being able to close
The flood gates when they are opened
I have settled for becoming a shell of a person
Because I am too afraid of who I am when
These walls I have built are broken down around me
    It is painful to have to choose
Between being asleep and never able to dream,
or to walk the world awake and face the nightmares.

No matter how many times it happens,
I am never prepared for when it gets bad.
There is no way to fully remember what it feels like
To experience the world in monochromatic stillness
Until it switches-
The way that all the senses are somehow leveled
To a painfully numbed baseline;
How the food I trick myself into eating has no texture,
Let alone taste.
How no bath is hot enough,
And the wind from the fan blows the hair on my arm
But I do not feel its chill.
There is an outward sense of apathy
Periodically broken by tears no one sees,
The only reason I know they are there
Is the dampened collar of my shirt
    It can be so maddening
To feel so subdued,
To feel a physical part of me is not present-
The part that wakes everything up.
I suck in my stomach while my eyes pry the bathroom mirror,
and my face remains slack as my mind claws itself to pieces.
    I am a passive witness to something terrible.

    When I am awake again,
and the colors have returned to my life,
I will think of the bad days
and say
"They didn't kill me"
And a voice deep inside will whisper
    "Yet."

Memories of people who are no longer in my life are like ghosts that haunt the house that is my head. With each drafty breeze comes their lives flooding back into my consciousness, a motion picture stuck on play of tainted days branded history. I have a terrible memory- I forget to take my medication, I'm always convinced its Friday, and sometimes I catch myself mid-sentence not knowing what I was just talking about. Yet somehow, I remember why you can't take hot showers, because the burning tap was used as punishment on your young skin. I remember your families vacation spot and the story of New Years Eve when you sang karaoke until the sun rose on a new beginning. I remember you bit your fingernails until they bled, and that I always carried band aids for you. I remember that I used to stay up until 3 am because I knew that if you hadn't called by then, that the nightmares hadn't gotten you. I remember you asked the street performer to sing that Ed Sheeran song for me and we slow danced on a sidewalk full of people. I remember that your little sister struggles with her friends not treating her right. I remember that you stayed up all night to make me laugh. And my memory may be poor, but I will never forget that you all said you'd stay.

The drive home becomes a blur of red lights and oncoming traffic,
Eyes glazed over as the trees roll by,
The songs play like static–
Folding into one another until
The hum in my ears is deafening.
The world is still as I accelerate;
My eyes remind themselves to blink.
    I could drive to the end of the world,
I have seen it.
    Yet I find myself parked,
With my head on the steering wheel,
Wondering how I got here
And why I feel like I missed my turn.

Loneliness can feel like drowning
You are trying so hard to swim,
To keep your head above the riptide,
Only to find that you are swallowing salt.
You feel as though you have swum the entire ocean,
Only to find you have been treading water.
Biologically, your body knows when to stop
Holding its breath
And so slowly
You succumb
To the dark

My head used to be filled with stories.
Where did they go?
Where did I go?

I see you everywhere
And I am scared to sleep
Because I know you will be there too.
It's been months
And I still check for your car
In every parking lot.
You are a ghost who haunts me,
The shadow I see in crowded rooms.
I want to forget your face
Your voice
Your hands
And I hate myself
Because I can't.

I fell in a forest of people,
and no one heard a sound.

I was drowning in a flood of memories you left behind, because even though you aren't here anymore you are still everywhere and I'm not sure how to swim when the water just keeps coming. I am trying to gather all the things that are important before the water swallows them up like your smile and your laugh and the advice you gave me about growing up. I'm not sure why I am crying, it doesn't stop the flood. I'm worried I will leave something behind. Soon enough the water is going to take it all away and it will be gone, and you will forever be missing. If only the current would bring you back, I would take your hand and we would fight this flood together and carry our memories in waterproof bags. But you're not here, and the water is overflowing. I am trying to catch the memories that are slipping under. I can't carry them all. I really have to leave now, before I drown in this misery. If I died here, I would join you, but who would catch our memories?

People don't tell you
That the ones you love most
Are the ones who will
Break your heart
    Their opinions
Weigh more
Their judgments
Stick within your mind
    Although you may
Love them
Adore them
They may never feel the same
    It's devestating
To be let down
Over
And over
    To open up only
To be shut down
By your
Beloved
    The devils in the details
But their feelings
Are written all over
Their face

I was cursed to be lonely for eternity. From a young age, watching other kids play on the playground I knew the yearning for connection. And the thing is, even at points in my life where my phone was constantly blowing up with texts and calls, I still felt empty. I feel as lonely at a party surrounded by people as I do in my dark bathroom in the tub. I push people away and wonder why I am alone when they leave. I try my best to be likable. I try my best to be kind. I have always felt like there is something inherently wrong with me to cycle through people like I do. When I make friends, I attach like a parasite and love them until they are drained. I don't know how to love a little. I only know grand gestures and diving headfirst and becoming a burden to those I love. I wish I knew how to be casual. I wish I understood how to not take everything so personally. I wish my texts being left on read didn't leave me feeling like that little girl, waiting for someone to pick her. I am too much and not enough all in the same breath. All I have ever wanted is to be loved. To be chosen first. To be thought of. And in the end, I will always be left heartbroken over people whose only crime was choosing someone else.

The internet tells me to love myself
With ads for Ozempic in the margins
    I twist and contort in the mirror
Trying to make myself thinner
    I have come to know my scale like a lover
Checking in multiple times a day
Missing it when I am away
Hoping one day it will change
    I hide myself behind baggy tshirts
And suck my stomach in when I enter a room
Because my sizes reputation precedes me
My body will always speak for me
It will introduce itself first
In every interaction it will be there
Taking up space
    I wish I could turn off this voice in my head
Because I know being skinny will not fix me
But desire is a powerful drug
And I am hooked on the rush of a growling stomach
    I hope one day I will be able to eat at a buffet
Or enjoy snacks at a party
But for now I am trying to unlearn the hate for myself
That blossomed the first time I was called fat
Like being fat was synonymous with being bad
    And maybe I will always be scared to ask for more
Or cry silently in a bathroom when someone says
"Wow you eat fast!"
I am holding out hope that my body will not always define me
And that One day I will be able to look in the mirror
And say that sacred word
    Beautiful.

I'm angry. I'm angry about the things that have happened to me. I am angry about the things happening in the world. I'm angry that other people aren't angry. I'm angry that I never got an apology. I'm angry that words said to me as a child still stick in my side like a thorn. I'm angry that I trusted you with my words and you threw them away. I'm angry that I never got a high school prom. I'm angry that I always try harder in relationships. I'm angry that I'm embarrassed to share my writing. I'm angry that I felt the need to sexualize myself in order to feel beautiful. I'm angry that people on the internet think because they have no profile picture that they can say whatever they want. I'm angry that my dog died. I'm angry that no one seems to notice when I am falling apart. I'm angry that you will never read this. I'm angry that there was no reason for Grandpa to have a heart attack, he just did. I'm angry that my body has sabotaged itself. I'm angry that no doctors take my pain seriously. I'm angry that I lost my teen years to depression. I'm angry that people hurt people. I'm angry that people preach love and spit bigotry in the same breath. I'm angry that people hurt animals. I'm angry that I will never be 16 again. I'm angry that I don't know if anyone will ever read my work. I'm angry that I'm a dreamer. I'm angry that I have so little self-worth that no matter what I do, I always self-sabotage. I am angry that politics are a popularity contest between career politicians. I'm angry that the cost of living is going up while the work force is tightening. I'm angry that COVID-19 happened. I'm angry for those years I spent holed up in my room. I'm angry that it took me so long to tell someone I was dying inside. I am angry that I am so angry. I want so desperately to let go, to let it all go. But I worry if I'm not angry, who will be? Who will step in and say something the next time they hear injustice? I don't want to be angry anymore. I am so tired. Please, let me be free from this constant fire in my chest. Please, let me rest.

My heart aches in ways I cannot put into words.
I have twisted and contorted trying to remold
Myself into something people will like.
I have read all the tips, tried all the advice
And yet I still end up lonely, every time.
I don't know how to say this, but I guess I will try;
I am drowning, and no one knows.
I am being swept out to sea and you
Are waving from the shore.
I am a candle burning out and you
Only see me for the smoke I leave behind.
I am a rainbow, something beautiful after the storm
But temporary- gone before you even think to capture it.
I am an old book that has been shelved for the last time,
Tuning into dust over centuries of neglect.
I am fading, is what I'm trying to say.
And as I lower the curtains on my life,
You will all applaud.

I am so scared
That everyone else
Feels the same way about me that I do

Part Two: Twilight

I sat by my window
Watching the seasons
Pass without me;
A passive participant in my own life
    I kept waiting for
The world to notice me
For someone
Anyone
To breathe life into my lungs
    Time passed
And with the closing of summer
I realized no one was coming to save me
    And so, I began planning my own rescue
    Because in the end,
I'm the only one who could.

    Staring at the ceiling
I can almost pretend I'm watching
The stars shooting across the night sky;
So many that I run out of wishes
I close my eyes,
Take a shuttering breath,
And list the reasons I have to stay
On my fingers
I make it to six before I stumble
And maybe that's God's way of telling me I will
Forever come up short
Nothing I do will ever fix these broken pieces that
Make up the fractured person I am
As I lie there,
succumbing to my anxieties,
I think of you.
I think of all the time you have held me when my world was turning
in on itself.
I feel the way you rub the pad of your thumb across my palm and tell
me it will be alright when morning comes.
I hear your voice as you tell me you love me
Over and over
And I wonder how I could ever leave this place with you standing by
my side
How could I promise you to fight and then swallow my demise in the
hours of the morning the sun doesn't touch?
I feel a curse weighing down my shoulders,
one that drove heroes to battle,
Teenagers to poison,
The moth to the light that turned out to be its gluttonous end.
I wonder if I will always think of my life as a movie in its final chap-
ter.

Or if one day I will lie in bed,
Just as I am today,
And lose count of how many reasons I have to stay.

Gordon
There's a feeling in my stomach
One that I can't place
It twists and it turns
When I think of your face
I think of your laughter
And your kind eyes
It feels like suffocating
When a friend dies
I'll miss you forever
This I know to be true
The world is already darker
Without someone like you

I go to the river to think
Or maybe to pray
It seems lately like I'm always talking to God
    I used to hate when the leaves would crumble off their branches,
I felt every year like a part of me died with them
    I close my eyes and listen to the rushing stream, and I
Recognize my own heartbeat in the current
    There are some people who are like water;
They slip between your fingertips the harder you try to hold them
    I ask God to stop the seasons
To let me swim in the summer sun one more day
And yet more leaves fall
And the wind becomes the ghost of a breeze on my face
And the stillness silences the forest
    I hate the sadness, but I understand her too.
    There is a time for rest,
A time for sleep,
And as the world around me changes,
How did I every expect to stay the same?

    Sometimes I miss the sadness.
I miss the crying on the shower floor,
The arguing on the phone
Followed by staring at my ceiling til the sun casts lilac light
Across my comforter in the early morning hours.
    Sometimes I miss the anger.
I miss screaming in my car until my throat ran dry
Or feeling the fire in my stomach begging to escape
My mouth in a storm of thunderous curse words and insults.
    Sometimes I miss the hurt.
I miss looking at my shoes and counting the times
The laces intertwined so that I did not look up and cry.
    I miss seeing the people I care about care about
Other people more than me
And that knot in my throat every time I have been called
Ugly.
    Sometimes I miss these things,
Because although they may be painful
And sour
And twisted
    To feel nothing at all is torture in itself.
I stare in the mirror at a person I do not know,
Yet she reflects my every move.
I hold my pills in my palm and consider pouring them back,
But remember the days I spent napping in a hospital gown
In a bed that was not my own.
    It is hard to fight for your wellbeing, only to be met
With your own indifference.
    Sometimes I miss the sadness
Because it gave me something to hold onto.

As I looked up
In the cold November sky
I mistook a plane
For a shooting star
    Once I realized my delusion,
A thick heaviness found home in my chest
Maybe because I no longer had the promise of a wish
Or possibly because I longed to be on that plane
Leaving the person I am scared of becoming behind,
Waving at her as the plane lifted off
Flying towards a future
Where I can meet my gaze in the mirror
And feel safe rather than swallowed whole by loneliness
    That's all a wish in itself, isn't it?
    To run away and lose all sense of our past lives-
Our short comings, fears, traumas
To erase the parts that make us feel less than whole
Who would I be if I cleansed my memory of the events
That have molded me?
    There are no answers
Only more questions
And so I lay back
And watch the sky

For those few minutes
With my headphones in
Body curled up beneath covers,
Alone in the room I spend all my days in,
I cease to exist.
I erase myself from reality
Removing all the trauma
And the pain
Along with the happiness and joy, too.
I strip away all that makes me human
And lie there
An untethered being
Bound by no memories or people
And for fleeting minutes
I am completely free.
For those moments frozen in that
Space of in between that only I can see
I am not the words people have
Pinned on me before I knew what I
Thought of myself
I am not the pain I have inflicted upon
MYself for nearly half my life
I am merely stripped down to a soul
Wandering through a doorway
Of possibility and loneliness
And trying to figure out how those coincide
When the music fades out
And I fade back in
I have to decide if I'm ready to try existing again
Some days I pull the covers up
And restart my playlist for the 100th time

    Other times
When I return
I am ready to start new.
    I just need to cease to exist for a little while
In order to come back
Alive

On nights like these,
When my thoughts swallow me like the pills I crave,
I close my eyes
Take a deep breath
And let myself feel weightless-
The burden of my illness no longer tugging at my shoulders.
I sink into the bathtub and pretend that I can
Drown out the thoughts
Picturing them sinking to the bottom of the ocean
Far
Far
Away.
I remember the days that weren't so dark
The days where I was held in the arms of someone
Who made all the pain worth it,
The days where my laughter drowned out the tears,
Days where I could see a future.
And for a while, I cease to exist.
I am gone, a mere ripple in time.
And when I'm ready,
I open my eyes and let the light slip in.

The last time I cried in my mother's arms
I was twenty two
I was still just the little girl who wanted people to want her
    I came to realize
After all those etars
That maybe I was meant to be lonely
    There is a sadness that plagues me
That weighs my shoulders down
That makes heartache feel like an open wound
    I've been taking my medication
But I still have the dreams
    I will always wonder
What I could have done
To deserve this curse of loneliness
    In the end I'm asking questions to a God
I'm not sure hears me anymore
    To be alone in a universe as giant as ours
Is to be like space itself:
So vast, yet so empty.

There are many things I wish I could tell you
Like how I still have nightmares
That make me hollow eyed throughout the day
    Or that sometimes. I feel things getting bad again
And I wonder if this is it
    I want to tell you that I am scared
Of a future I have never planned for
One I never let myself dream of
    I wish you knew I don't expect you to stay
I know it's a bad habit
But I am so used to people leaving
    There are so many other things
Things I don't think will ever leave my mouth
You may find them in my silence
Or perhaps
Between these pages

I want to be a poet
More than I want
Breath in my lungs

Maybe that's the problem
    I would die
Just for you
To understand me

I often wonder where you are,
If you made it out.
I think of all the laughter we shared
On those late nights
Where sleep evaded us.
I remember how red your face gets
When you are angry,
How good you were at cooking,
And how for as long as I knew you
You wanted to be anyone but yourself.
We were electric,
We were so vivacious and alive,
Until one day...
We weren't.
We weren't anything anymore.
And I am still trying to understand
How to live in a world where you are not my friend
And we are not each other's good morning text
And goodnight call.
We walked through the fire together,
But I was the one who got burned.

I rip myself open through poetry
And let the sadness and frustration
Pour out of me in stanzas
My tears blur the ink
On my journal pages
    I have never known how to be subtle.
    I write because my thoughts
Are too much to keep inside.
They beat at my brain
Like crazed animals in a cage,
Violent, yet scared of the way
The world will see them.

I used to think that I would wake up one day and be better
That I would roll out of bed free of my depression
I would get up and brush my teeth with no anxiety
And eat breakfast without thinking about calories
    I used to think it wouldn't happen to me
That I could never end up hospitalized
That I would never be on a medication schedule
That I would never take a blade to my body
    I used to think I could make it go away
That I could put on a smile
That I could say "I ate at someone else's house"
That I couldn't tell anyone
    I used to think I was alone
That my parents didn't understand
And my friends would think I was crazy
That no one had ever felt like me
    I used to think all of those things
And lived my life believing the lies
My brain fabricated
    I now know that I never walk alone
and I cannot let others
either

Nostalgia can be painful in the way it makes us see memories through rose-colored glasses. I often find myself yearning for a time many years ago when things were 'better', but I seem to forget the reality of those years. My teenage years were spent trying to survive my own mind every day. I fought to get out of bed, get to school, and keep friends. I look back and see the laughter and the good times and wish I could go back but to be honest, I'm not sure I would make it if I went back. Those were the bad years. Those were the years I spent every night up until 4 am crying silently in my bed, listening to music on repeat and convincing myself I had something to live for. Those were the years that I had to wear shorts to the pool or the beach because I couldn't let anyone see what I had done to my own body. Those were the years I would try and eat as little as possible because maybe if I was smaller, I would be happier. Those were the years I got hurt and so I turned around and hurt others. I hurt the people I loved most. Those were the years I was so insecure in myself I ruined friendships and tore up everything and everyone who wanted to help me. Those years were not beautiful. Depression is not beautiful. It is all consuming. It is exhaustion, headaches, joint pain, and stress acne. Your own mind convinces you to press the self-destruct button.

If I could tell myself something that I know now, it will not hurt this much forever. Between hospitals and residential treatment and therapy and medication you will find it easier to meet your eyes in the mirror. You will wake up and be excited for the day. I wish I could say it goes away entirely, and who knows, maybe someday it will. But I am 12 years deep into this battle and on the good days I have come to terms with the fact that I may have to fight for the rest of my life, and on the bad days I can't imagine taking this pain a second longer. It's all about perspective. Today was a bad day. Maybe tomorrow will be too.

But I'd like the chance to find out, and so I'll stay.

I used to think that I would not survive without you.
That to lose you would be to lose myself.
But you are gone,
And I am still here,
The sun is still rising on a brighter tomorrow,
One I never thought I'd see.
    I am aching,
I am bleeding,
but I am here.
    And every day I walk without you
Is a day that I feel stronger
Because I have come to realize
I loved the version of you I came to know
At 15 when the nights were dark
And you would show your scars
And I would show mine
    How did we not see that we were still bleeding?
    Every poke,
Every prod,
Of open wounds...
We thought we were each other's savior.
    But all you ever taught me is you can only save yourself.

And so, you're gone,
and I am still here,
Wondering when the phantom pain will stop.

I write because it is the only thing that makes sense
When the waters are rising, and I feel I might drown
Or when I took at my hands and realize they are bloody
I turn to a paper and pen to make the hurt go away
As if I could take all this pain welling up inside me
And spill it across pages of sloppy scrawl
And all the hurt and all the tears would simply dissolve
I write because I feel I have no other choice
The words pour out of me in one way or another
On napkins, business cards, receipts
I cannot contain them
They have a mind of their own
And they are begging to be released
I write because it is the only thing that has never left
No matter the sadness
No matter the drama
I have always been able to open a document
and bleed

Blow out your candles
Close your eyes and make the wish
The one you have made 10 years in a row
One that you are not sure will ever come true
But you are holding out hope for
Smell the smoke as they flicker out
Take a deep breath of the charged air
Maybe this will be the year
Things change

There is so much I want to say to you.
There are so many moments I look for you
In a crowded room. I hear good news and think
To call you, but quickly remember we don't do that
Anymore.
    We don't do anything anymore.
    Maybe I will always regret the way we fizzled out,
Preferring a fiery explosion to drifting apart.
It has been one whole year and I still
Hurt when people say your name in conversation
As though I am not healing, as though what we had
Was casual. I hate that we ended in a place of
Bitterness and anger, but maybe that is how it was always
Going to end.
    You, dazzling for others, and me chasing my dreams
That you could not be a part of.
    So, this is my goodbye to you, to us.
To all the late-night phone calls
And inside jokes. I now lay us to rest,
Burying what I once thought would last a lifetime.
I will dig a hole and put this hatchet within
And cover it with tear-soaked soil.
    And that will be that.
We will be dead to the world,
Scripture written on a headstone reading
"They once thought they had it all."

Do all prayers reach heaven?
Do the backseat pleas ever bother God?
Has He heard the cries I have sent from my bedside?
    I don't know.
Is anyone listening?
Is anyone out there at all?
    The fear that I am talking to no one
Is greater than the fear that an almighty
Someone is listening in.
    My knees are bruised from kneeling to pray
My hands are aching from being clasped so tightly
My eyes are swollen from crying into my palms
    I'm not saying I need a miracle
Lord knows I don't deserve one
I'm just asking for a sign
    A message to let me know You're here
Something to let me know
I'm not alone.

This one is for you
For the one who feels invisible
For the one who thinks their only option is leaving.
For the one who was always picked last.
For the one that laughs hard and cries harder.
For the one who feels they will never be enough.
For the one who has given everything.
For the one who has received nothing.
For the one who still clings to a little bit of hope.
For the one who is scared of what comes next.
For the one who feels like a burden.
For the one who tells themselves they are worthless.
For the one who is losing touch with reality.
For the one who is ready to go.
    I see you.
You are not alone.
Turn your pain into purpose
Be your own reason for waking up.
    This life can be painful,
But it would be so much more painful
Without you.

Part 3: Sunrise

I decided to disappear one day,
To close the blinds and leave my passions behind.
And though my body was physically absent from
A world of pain and let-downs,
My mind still screamed relentlessly,
Trying to get out and make change.
But how can I change the world
If I can't even change myself?
If I have learned one thing it is that
If you wait for the time to be right
You will be waiting forever.
So, I open the blinds and face the sunshine
And take a step into the light.

The sound of my voice singing along to the radio in my car
Sounds like a victory cry
I have stared silently at the road for three months
And the sound of my song
Startles me
She has been gone for so long
I forgot what she sounded like
I cross my fingers and pray the music never stops again

There is something powerful in kindness,
Something rebellious in the choice
To turn a blind eye to evil,
To reach out a hand and say
"Me too."

She is kind.
She walks gently on tattered soil
And prays every animal goes to heaven.
    She is patient.
She leans in when things get tough
And will hold your hand no matter how sweaty.
    She reminds you that there are reasons to stay alive.
She has battle scars to prove
That not every fight is won easily.
    She is loud.
She dances with her arms up
And sings loudly off key in her car.
    She is free.
She walks into a room knowing exactly
Who she is.
    She is alive.
That in itself is her own little victory against the world,
One that she relishes in every morning.
    She is grateful.
She lies awake and counts off all the things that make her happy,
Eventually sleeping a dreamless sleep.
    She is content.
The world may have turned its back on her,
But she never turned her back on the world.
    And that is what makes her extraordinary.

01.01.2020

Watching the ball drop on the closing of the decade
Feels foreign to people who thought
they would not be around to see it.
Fireworks and confetti blast off into
A future that is now alive and tangible.
We hug each other in silence and let the colorful sky
Be the funeral for our past, we don't need it here.

Ask me the meaning of life and I will
Respond with love
Every
Single
Time.

My hands may shake,
But I am steady.

The nights are hard.
When the lights go out and the world
Closes its eyes, mine stay open.
The shadows stretch across the ceiling,
Swallowing me whole beneath my covers.
My bathroom floor has become a refuge.
I know there are others like me-
People who spend their nights
On the brink of self-destruction,
People who have to talk themselves
Into living just to make it through the night.
    My advice to you
Is to stay til sunrise
Because the world is a lot less scary
When you can see the light.

You have forgotten me,
But I will always remember
Your perfume and cigarettes
And how you made me want to get better.

You and I will one day be a memory
And maybe that makes you sad
But what an honor it is to witness
The changing of the skies at sunrise
To hold the hand of a lover
To disappear under the waves of the ocean
To scream until there is no air in your lungs
To speed down dirt roads
To cry at funerals
To dance until your feet hurt-
    What an honor it is
To be alive

When I can't sleep at night
I like to talk to God
And ask him for forgiveness
For not being the perfect daughter
For not bruising my knees at the alter
For swearing in his name
For sleeping through my Sunday alarms
    I'd like to think he's listening
    I'd like to think he forgives me

;

I used to count down from ten
On my fingers of reasons
To stay alive
I'd make it to five,
Maybe six,
Before fizzling out
And staring at the ceiling
Wondering where I had gone wrong
What had I done to
Deserve a life of broken promises
And strained relationships?
Why was I made to compare myself,
To question every compliment?
What had gone so wrong in
My creation that I wanted to die
Every morning when my eyes opened?
These are the questions I have asked myself
Thousands of times
In the middle of the night
On the bus to school
Lying on the cool floor of a friend's bathroom
I have found with time
And heartbreak
That I was not made to suffer,
But to feel so deeply
And love so intensely
That sometimes I am misunderstood.
    Maybe it is not a curse
To have the world push you
Down again
And again
Because only then do you

Have the chance
To make them watch
As you rise.
    If you say something enough times,
You start to believe it.
    At least that's what I've been told.
    So here I sit,
Eyes squeezed shut,
Fists gripped tightly
Whispering
    I am Beautiful
    I am Beautiful
    I am beautiful

I would not be here if it were not for you.
I don't tell you that I love you enough,
You show me the best parts of myself
And don't run away at the worst ones.
    You held my hand
When I walked through Hell
And lost myself
    And you were there when I made it back home
I never told you that you were my rock
But through all those years
You were my anchor, keeping me at shore
When all I wanted was to drift away.
    Thank you.

They say my poetry is 'too sad'
"Where is the happy ending?"
"This doesn't help anyone"
    But what they don't understand
Is depression is not something
You 'make it out of'
    Recovery is a lifelong process
    It's going years without
Self-injury
But still having it cross your mind
Because for so long
It was your solution
It was your safety
    Its suicide being your solution
To the littlest things
Even when you are feeling happy
    It's taking medication to
Balance the chemicals in your brain
Every day for the rest of your life
    So no
    My poetry doesn't wrap up nicely
Mental health is not pretty
Or aesthetic
    It's survival.
    And there is no room for lies
When helping others survive.

I hope you know it's okay to cry. I hope you know it's okay if today wasn't a good day. Not every day is going to be the best. Keep going anyway. I hope you learn to love yourself for who you are. I hope you can look in the mirror without tearing yourself apart. I hope you can pick out an outfit without crying. I hope you know you don't have to be strong all the time. I hope you know that you are the one in control. I hope you smiled today. I hope that reoccurring nightmare goes away. I hope your friend texts you first. I hope it's sunny on you Birthday. I hope you know that your pain will not last forever. I hope you know that you are allowed to feel happiness within all of this darkness. I hope you remember who you are, the real you. Not the depression, you.

I hope you remember I am rooting for you.

I hope you remember these words when you need them most.

I hope you never need them.

The sun will shine on us again
Maybe tomorrow
Maybe in the next lifetime
But we will feel its rays
And its warmth against our skin
And forgive ourselves
For all that we did not become.

It's strange living to see things you never thought you'd get the chance to. At eleven years old I would close my eyes and hope and pray that I would not wake up again. This went on for years, blowing out birthday candles and crossing my fingers that something would give. I felt that I could not bend, I could only break. I lived this way, walking on a tightrope of sanity until I stumbled and felt what it was like to free fall. I have written so many goodbye letters. I've drawn up legal documents of who is to speak for me if I am unable. I have broken so many promises. Really, I don't feel like I deserve this hundredth chance I have been given at life. I don't understand it and may spend the rest of my life trying to discover why I made it, and others didn't. But my birthday is in two weeks and my mind is not preoccupied with thoughts of dying. Winter has come, and I can feel the cold. I am planning my wedding. I graduate college in just five months. I look at all that I have withstood and all the pain I have made it through and have to remind myself that I did that. That was me. I fought through those lonely nights, I spent those days in the hospital, I ripped up those letters that I never sent. So now when I slip, I remember how many times I have done this before and how many times I have gotten back up. I think of how many times I have picked up the pieces and started over again. I think of how tired I am, and how despite the fatigue, I am grateful to feel anything at all. I think of all the reasons I have to stay down and give up, but still I rise.

I have heard it all before
Tell me why we can't hang out
Because your mom thinks I'll
"give you my depression"
      Tell me people who self-harm are crazy
As I grip my leg under the table
      Tell me all about the 'loony bin'
And I'll tell you the real stories
Of those who end up hospitalized
      Tell me therapy is useless
And I will recount how it saved my life

      Tell me how it never gets better
And I will prove you wrong.

Dear Younger Me,

They will tell you that you are too loud. They will tell you that you are too big. They will make you laugh just to mimic the sound. You will ask yourself every day "What is wrong with me?" You will sit alone on the playground and watch other kids playing tag or spilling secrets and feel a pain deep inside your chest. This is an ache you will know your whole life. You will grow attached to your friends and as you get older, they will grow attached to other people. It's okay to cry. I know you loved them. You cannot hold onto people who do not hold on to you. As you grow older the weight in your chest will turn into a monster that follows you wherever you go. It will hold your hand and tell you it knows best-don't listen. It's a liar. It will place a blade in your hand and tell you where to strike. For a long time, it will feel like your only friend. I know it's hard. I know how lonely you are. But you have to keep going. If not for yourself, for mom and dad. If not for them, for your brother. Your grandmas. Your internet friends. The promise of a sunrise tomorrow. Get in bed and count to the highest number you can until you stop crying. Breathe. I know you are tired. I know no one understands, how could they? Yes, you eventually tell mom. She's terrified. Not of you, but for you. Hold on to mom and dad, they will do anything to help you get better. You have to tell them, though. It is killing you to keep it all inside. The monster will morph and grow and change over the years, but its voice will stay the same. You will never be enough for it. You will be unlovable, worthless. No matter how hard you try. You will carry scars that no one will ever see. You will spend more time in doctors' offices and therapists' couches than in high school. You will want to give up more times than you can physically count. But you will make it through every trial, every hardship. You will hit rock bottom and stand up, dust yourself off, and start climbing again. You will see the mountain tops. You will fall in love. You will never rid yourself of the monster, but you will learn to quiet it.

What I really want to say is don't give up. Not now, not ever.
Keep going.

Hole up in bed
Squeeze your eyes shut
Count by 3's to the
Highest number you can.
Remember the rule:
You can't get out of bed
Until the sun is up.
Nothing good happens
In the quiet of the night.
So pull the covers up
And start counting again
If you lose your place
Take a deep breath
And start over
3…6…9…12…15…18…

There are so many people I want to hug one more time
So many stories I have held space for
So many tears I have shared with others in rooms
Where the walls are heavy with secrets
        They may not know it
But their bravery saved my life
Their willingness to commit to recovery
Changed my outlook
        Their perseverance through hell itself
Made me fall in love with people
I have heard stories that have made me sob
I have held hands with souls
Wrapped in fresh bandages
        I have shared laughter and meals
With people just like me
        I wish you could see it-
Us laughing around a table,
Our souls just an ounce lighter
From realizing
We are never alone

100 Reasons to Stay Alive (In no Particular Order):

1. The smell of old books
2. Cold water on a hot day
3. Dancing with no pants on
4. New songs you will love
5. Sunflower fields in the summer
6. Looking around at a concert and feeling like you belong
7. Cute stickers
8. Cat paws
9. Laughing until your stomach hurts
10. Funny thrift store finds
11. Hugs from your favorite people
12. Staying up late talking to someone on the phone
13. The lights at Christmas time
14. Stomach drops on rollercoasters
15. Losing yourself in a story
16. Making new friends
17. Stupid tattoos
18. Dogs getting excited when you walk in the room
19. Giving gifts
20. Burping when your stomach hurts and feeling better
21. Obsessing over a movie
22. Hearing how different people sneeze
23. Carving pumpkins with funny faces
24. Telling a story that makes people laugh
25. Seeing a full moon
26. Weird celestial events (i.e. solar eclipse)
27. Kissing someone you love
28. Getting a good fortune from a fortune cookie
29. Catching a shirt from a t-shirt cannon
30. Watching your favorite team win
31. Finding clothes that fit you perfectly
32. Funny grandma Facebook posts

33. Listening to little kids explain something wrong
34. Rainbows
35. DOUBLE RAINBOWS
36. Seeing a new place
37. Overhearing funny conversations
38. Sending memes to a friend
39. Camping under the stars
40. Seeing a live performance
41. Dramatically reading old poetry
42. Learning something new
43. Watching someone you love grow up
44. The chance your favorite band COULD get back together
45. Mooing at cows who moo back at you
46. Watching chickens move their heads in funny ways
47. Looking in an animal's eyes and feeling like they understand you
48. Spring cleaning
49. Receiving a genuine compliment
50. Sending snail mail
51. Writing poetry
52. Magic shows
53. Looking at drunk selfies you took
54. Seeing the leaves change color
55. Freshly baked cookies
56. Finishing a big book
57. Feeling proud of yourself
58. Seeing a shooting star
59. Making new favorite memories
60. Looking through old photographs
61. Rediscovering a passion
62. Watching a mind-blowing documentary
63. Helping someone
64. Singing in the car
65. Having someone remember a small detail about you
66. The smell of rain

67. Seeing a random act of kindness
68. Conversations with strangers that make you feel connected
69. Walking on soft grass with bare feet
70. Finding something to believe in
71. Running until you're gasping for air
72. Smiling at babies
73. Babies smiling at you
74. Free little libraries
75. Figuring out the solution to a problem
76. Dreaming of your ideal future
77. The sound of frogs singing at night
78. Waking up before the sun
79. The view from the top of a mountain
80. Road trips
81. Finding a character you relate to
82. Orange juice on a sore throat
83. Being recognized for your hard work
84. Sleepovers with friends
85. Wind blowing your hair with the car windows down
86. The moment right before you fall asleep
87. The pure spirit of animals
88. Traveling to a new place
89. Waking up in a hotel knowing the day is going to be exciting
90. The quiet of being alone
91. Sitting in the shower
92. Dancing in the rain
93. Feeling better after being sick
94. Silly faces snuck between friends
95. Your favorite food, just how you like it
96. Someone holding your hand
97. Hearing an old favorite song
98. Sitting by a campfire
99. Funny jokes
100. Realizing you were enough all along

Acknowledgments

There are so many people I want to thank when it comes to *Stay Til Sunrise*. If you have been a positive force in my life at any point since 2019, consider yourself acknowledged. Seriously, thank you. I could not have done this without you.

I'd like to thank my Mom and Dad for never giving up on me. They have shown me time and time again that they would do anything to keep me going and I truly cannot thank you guys enough. I can 100% without a doubt say I would not be here today without your support and love.

I would like to thank my love, Mitchell, for being my biggest fan and constantly pushing me to follow my dreams. You have shown me that I am capable of great things. I love you.

Thank you to my amazing friends over the years (this is where the naming will get dicey, I'm so sorry if you are left out!) - Kaitlyn, Maddie, Brian, Josie, Autumn, Anja, Kimberly, Angel, Jasmine, Nicholas, Zach, McKenzie, Spencer, Lex, Beau, Shalia, Kayla, Madelyn, Ashley, Adrianna...so many more. Thank you.

To the educators who changed my life—Lori, Tasha, and Jill. You know who you are. Thank you for believing in me and helping me through some of my hardest years.

Thank you to my family; Jake and Kristi for the constant memes, and for everyone who has supported my writing and my mental health journey over the years. I love you all.

And thank you, dear reader. For giving me a chance. For listening to my deepest thoughts and feelings. For believing in me.

In honor of Gordon Corsetti. Gone too soon. I know you would have loved this one. I promised I would keep your message alive. I hope I made you proud.

www.ingramcontent.com/pod-product-compliance
Lightning Source LLC
Chambersburg PA
CBHW070550160726
48003CB00005B/1983